50 Creative Uses for Leftover Ingredients

By: Kelly Johnson

Table of Contents

- Vegetable Stock
- Bread Crumbs
- Fruit Smoothies
- Frittatas
- Pasta Salad
- Rice Bowls
- Quiche
- Soup
- Casserole
- Stir-Fry
- Chili
- Baked Potatoes
- Pancakes
- Granola Bars
- Salad Dressing
- Pasta Bake
- Stuffed Peppers
- Savory Oatmeal
- Ice Cream Topping
- Homemade Pizza
- Smoothie Bowl
- Bread Pudding
- Vegetable Chips
- Marinade
- Dips
- Crispy Tacos
- Fruit Salad
- Energy Bites
- Savory Muffins
- Frozen Smoothie Packs
- Coconut Rice
- Homemade Croutons
- Veggie Burgers
- Noodle Salad
- Fruit Infused Water

- Nut Milk
- Pickles
- Cake Pops
- Herb Butter
- Savory Rice Cakes
- Baked Goods
- Egg Drop Soup
- Homemade Dog Treats
- Potato Pancakes
- Stuffed Zucchini
- Chowder
- Fruit Leather
- Frozen Snacks
- Scones
- Savory Rice Pilaf

Vegetable Stock

Ingredients:

- 1 onion, quartered
- 2 carrots, chopped
- 2 celery stalks, chopped
- 4 cloves garlic, smashed
- 1 bay leaf
- 1 tsp black peppercorns
- 6 cups water
- Fresh herbs (like thyme and parsley)

Instructions:

1. In a large pot, combine all ingredients and bring to a boil.
2. Reduce heat and let simmer for 45 minutes to 1 hour.
3. Strain the stock through a fine-mesh sieve, discarding solids.
4. Let cool and store in the refrigerator or freezer.

Bread Crumbs

Ingredients:

- 4 slices of stale bread (any kind)

Instructions:

1. Preheat the oven to 350°F (175°C).
2. Tear bread into small pieces and spread on a baking sheet.
3. Bake for 10-15 minutes until dry and lightly toasted.
4. Allow to cool, then pulse in a food processor until fine.
5. Store in an airtight container.

Fruit Smoothies

Ingredients:

- 1 banana
- 1 cup frozen berries (strawberries, blueberries, or mixed)
- 1 cup yogurt (or non-dairy alternative)
- 1/2 cup milk (or non-dairy alternative)
- 1 tbsp honey or maple syrup (optional)

Instructions:

1. In a blender, combine all ingredients.
2. Blend until smooth, adjusting the consistency with more milk if necessary.
3. Pour into glasses and serve immediately.

Frittatas

Ingredients:

- 6 eggs
- 1/2 cup milk
- 1 cup vegetables (like spinach, bell peppers, or onions), sautéed
- 1 cup cheese (like cheddar or feta), grated
- Salt and pepper to taste

Instructions:

1. Preheat the oven to 375°F (190°C).
2. In a bowl, whisk together eggs, milk, salt, and pepper.
3. Stir in the sautéed vegetables and cheese.
4. Pour the mixture into a greased oven-safe skillet.
5. Bake for 20-25 minutes until set and golden on top.
6. Let cool slightly before slicing and serving.

Pasta Salad

Ingredients:

- 2 cups cooked pasta (any shape)
- 1 cup cherry tomatoes, halved
- 1/2 cup cucumber, diced
- 1/4 cup red onion, finely chopped
- 1/4 cup olives, sliced
- 1/4 cup Italian dressing

Instructions:

1. In a large bowl, combine cooked pasta, tomatoes, cucumber, red onion, and olives.
2. Drizzle with Italian dressing and toss to coat.
3. Chill in the refrigerator for at least 30 minutes before serving.

Rice Bowls

Ingredients:

- 2 cups cooked rice (brown or white)
- 1 cup vegetables (like bell peppers, broccoli, or carrots), steamed or sautéed
- Protein of choice (like chicken, tofu, or beans)
- Soy sauce or teriyaki sauce for drizzling
- Green onions or sesame seeds for garnish

Instructions:

1. In bowls, layer cooked rice, vegetables, and protein.
2. Drizzle with soy sauce or teriyaki sauce.
3. Garnish with green onions or sesame seeds before serving.

Quiche

Ingredients:

- 1 pre-made pie crust
- 4 eggs
- 1 cup milk
- 1 cup vegetables (like spinach, mushrooms, or broccoli), sautéed
- 1 cup cheese (like Swiss or cheddar), grated
- Salt and pepper to taste

Instructions:

1. Preheat the oven to 375°F (190°C).
2. In a bowl, whisk together eggs, milk, salt, and pepper.
3. Stir in sautéed vegetables and cheese.
4. Pour the mixture into the pie crust.
5. Bake for 30-35 minutes until set and golden.
6. Let cool slightly before slicing and serving.

Soup

Ingredients:

- 1 onion, chopped
- 2 carrots, diced
- 2 celery stalks, diced
- 4 cloves garlic, minced
- 6 cups vegetable or chicken broth
- 1 can (14.5 oz) diced tomatoes
- 1 cup green beans, trimmed and chopped
- Salt and pepper to taste
- Fresh herbs (like thyme or parsley)

Instructions:

1. In a large pot, sauté onion, carrots, and celery until soft.
2. Add garlic and cook for another minute.
3. Pour in broth and diced tomatoes, bringing to a boil.
4. Add green beans and simmer for 15-20 minutes.
5. Season with salt, pepper, and fresh herbs before serving.

Casserole

Ingredients:

- 2 cups cooked pasta (like penne or rotini)
- 2 cups cooked vegetables (like broccoli, peas, or bell peppers)
- 2 cups shredded cheese (like cheddar or mozzarella)
- 1 can (10.5 oz) cream of mushroom soup
- 1/2 cup milk
- 1/2 cup breadcrumbs

Instructions:

1. Preheat the oven to 350°F (175°C).
2. In a large bowl, mix pasta, vegetables, cheese, soup, and milk.
3. Pour the mixture into a greased baking dish.
4. Top with breadcrumbs and extra cheese if desired.
5. Bake for 25-30 minutes until bubbly and golden.

Stir-Fry

Ingredients:

- 2 cups mixed vegetables (like bell peppers, broccoli, and snap peas)
- 1 lb protein (chicken, beef, tofu, or shrimp)
- 3 tbsp soy sauce
- 2 tbsp sesame oil
- 1 tbsp garlic, minced
- 1 tbsp ginger, minced
- Cooked rice or noodles for serving

Instructions:

1. Heat sesame oil in a large skillet or wok over medium-high heat.
2. Add garlic and ginger, sautéing for about 30 seconds.
3. Add protein and cook until browned.
4. Add mixed vegetables and stir-fry until tender-crisp.
5. Pour in soy sauce and toss to combine. Serve over rice or noodles.

Chili

Ingredients:

- 1 lb ground beef or turkey
- 1 onion, chopped
- 2 cloves garlic, minced
- 1 can (14.5 oz) diced tomatoes
- 1 can (15 oz) kidney beans, drained and rinsed
- 1 can (15 oz) black beans, drained and rinsed
- 2 tbsp chili powder
- 1 tsp cumin
- Salt and pepper to taste

Instructions:

1. In a large pot, brown the meat over medium heat.
2. Add onion and garlic, cooking until soft.
3. Stir in diced tomatoes, beans, chili powder, cumin, salt, and pepper.
4. Bring to a boil, then reduce heat and simmer for 30-40 minutes.
5. Serve hot, garnished with toppings like cheese or sour cream if desired.

Baked Potatoes

Ingredients:

- 4 large russet potatoes
- Olive oil
- Salt
- Toppings of choice (butter, sour cream, cheese, chives, etc.)

Instructions:

1. Preheat the oven to 425°F (220°C).
2. Scrub the potatoes and poke holes in them with a fork.
3. Rub with olive oil and sprinkle with salt.
4. Place on a baking sheet and bake for 45-60 minutes until tender.
5. Cut open and top with desired toppings before serving.

Pancakes

Ingredients:

- 1 cup all-purpose flour
- 2 tbsp sugar
- 1 tbsp baking powder
- 1/2 tsp salt
- 1 cup milk
- 1 egg
- 2 tbsp melted butter
- Maple syrup for serving

Instructions:

1. In a bowl, whisk together flour, sugar, baking powder, and salt.
2. In another bowl, combine milk, egg, and melted butter.
3. Pour the wet ingredients into the dry ingredients and stir until just combined.
4. Heat a non-stick skillet over medium heat. Pour 1/4 cup of batter for each pancake.
5. Cook until bubbles form on the surface, then flip and cook until golden. Serve with maple syrup.

Granola Bars

Ingredients:

- 2 cups rolled oats
- 1/2 cup nut butter (like almond or peanut)
- 1/4 cup honey or maple syrup
- 1/2 cup nuts and seeds (like almonds, sunflower seeds, or pumpkin seeds)
- 1/2 cup dried fruit (like raisins or cranberries)
- 1/2 tsp vanilla extract

Instructions:

1. Preheat the oven to 350°F (175°C).
2. In a large bowl, combine oats, nut butter, honey, nuts, dried fruit, and vanilla.
3. Press the mixture into a greased baking dish evenly.
4. Bake for 15-20 minutes until golden.
5. Allow to cool completely before cutting into bars.

Salad Dressing

Ingredients:

- 1/4 cup olive oil
- 2 tbsp balsamic vinegar
- 1 tsp Dijon mustard
- 1 clove garlic, minced
- Salt and pepper to taste

Instructions:

1. In a small bowl, whisk together olive oil, balsamic vinegar, Dijon mustard, and garlic.
2. Season with salt and pepper to taste.
3. Drizzle over your favorite salad and toss to coat.

Pasta Bake

Ingredients:

- 3 cups cooked pasta (like penne or rotini)
- 2 cups marinara sauce
- 1 cup ricotta cheese
- 1 cup shredded mozzarella cheese
- 1/2 cup grated Parmesan cheese
- 1 tsp Italian seasoning
- Salt and pepper to taste

Instructions:

1. Preheat the oven to 350°F (175°C).
2. In a large bowl, mix cooked pasta, marinara sauce, ricotta cheese, Italian seasoning, salt, and pepper.
3. Transfer the mixture to a greased baking dish.
4. Top with shredded mozzarella and Parmesan cheese.
5. Bake for 25-30 minutes until bubbly and golden.

Stuffed Peppers

Ingredients:

- 4 bell peppers, halved and seeds removed
- 1 lb ground beef or turkey
- 1 cup cooked rice
- 1 can (14.5 oz) diced tomatoes
- 1 cup shredded cheese (like cheddar or mozzarella)
- 1 tsp Italian seasoning
- Salt and pepper to taste

Instructions:

1. Preheat the oven to 375°F (190°C).
2. In a skillet, cook the ground meat until browned.
3. Stir in cooked rice, diced tomatoes, Italian seasoning, salt, and pepper.
4. Fill each pepper half with the meat mixture.
5. Place in a baking dish and top with shredded cheese.
6. Bake for 25-30 minutes until peppers are tender.

Savory Oatmeal

Ingredients:

- 1 cup rolled oats
- 2 cups vegetable or chicken broth
- 1/2 cup cooked vegetables (like spinach, mushrooms, or tomatoes)
- 1 egg (poached or fried)
- Salt and pepper to taste
- Optional toppings: cheese, avocado, or hot sauce

Instructions:

1. In a saucepan, bring broth to a boil.
2. Add oats and reduce heat to a simmer, cooking for 5-7 minutes until creamy.
3. Stir in cooked vegetables, salt, and pepper.
4. Serve topped with a poached or fried egg and any additional toppings.

Ice Cream Topping

Ingredients:

- 1 cup chocolate chips
- 1/2 cup heavy cream
- 1/4 cup chopped nuts (like almonds or walnuts)
- 1/4 cup caramel sauce

Instructions:

1. In a small saucepan, heat heavy cream over low heat until just simmering.
2. Remove from heat and stir in chocolate chips until melted and smooth.
3. Serve over ice cream with chopped nuts and a drizzle of caramel sauce.

Homemade Pizza

Ingredients:

- 1 pizza dough (store-bought or homemade)
- 1/2 cup marinara sauce
- 1 1/2 cups shredded mozzarella cheese
- Toppings of choice (like pepperoni, vegetables, or olives)
- Olive oil for brushing

Instructions:

1. Preheat the oven to 475°F (245°C).
2. Roll out the pizza dough on a floured surface to your desired thickness.
3. Transfer to a greased baking sheet or pizza stone.
4. Spread marinara sauce over the dough, leaving a border.
5. Sprinkle with mozzarella and add toppings.
6. Brush the crust with olive oil and bake for 12-15 minutes until golden and cheese is bubbly.

Smoothie Bowl

Ingredients:

- 1 frozen banana
- 1 cup frozen berries (like strawberries or blueberries)
- 1/2 cup yogurt or non-dairy alternative
- 1/2 cup milk or non-dairy alternative
- Toppings: sliced fruits, granola, seeds, or nuts

Instructions:

1. In a blender, combine frozen banana, frozen berries, yogurt, and milk.
2. Blend until smooth and thick, adding more milk if needed.
3. Pour into a bowl and top with your choice of fruits, granola, seeds, or nuts.

Bread Pudding

Ingredients:

- 4 cups cubed stale bread
- 2 cups milk
- 3 eggs
- 1/2 cup sugar
- 1 tsp vanilla extract
- 1 tsp cinnamon
- Optional: raisins or chocolate chips

Instructions:

1. Preheat the oven to 350°F (175°C).
2. In a bowl, whisk together milk, eggs, sugar, vanilla, and cinnamon.
3. Add cubed bread and stir until soaked.
4. If using, fold in raisins or chocolate chips.
5. Pour into a greased baking dish and bake for 30-35 minutes until set.

Vegetable Chips

Ingredients:

- 2 cups thinly sliced vegetables (like zucchini, sweet potatoes, or kale)
- 1 tbsp olive oil
- Salt and seasonings (like paprika or garlic powder)

Instructions:

1. Preheat the oven to 375°F (190°C).
2. Toss vegetable slices in olive oil, salt, and seasonings.
3. Spread in a single layer on a baking sheet.
4. Bake for 15-20 minutes until crispy, flipping halfway through.
5. Allow to cool and enjoy as a crunchy snack.

Marinade

Ingredients:

- 1/4 cup olive oil
- 1/4 cup soy sauce
- 2 tbsp vinegar (balsamic or apple cider)
- 2 tbsp honey or maple syrup
- 3 cloves garlic, minced
- 1 tsp ginger, grated
- Salt and pepper to taste

Instructions:

1. In a bowl, whisk together all ingredients until well combined.
2. Use immediately or store in the refrigerator for up to a week.
3. Marinate proteins or vegetables for at least 30 minutes before cooking.

Dips

Ingredients:

- 1 can (15 oz) chickpeas, drained and rinsed
- 1/4 cup tahini
- 2 tbsp olive oil
- 2 tbsp lemon juice
- 2 cloves garlic, minced
- Salt and pepper to taste
- Optional: spices like cumin or paprika

Instructions:

1. In a food processor, combine chickpeas, tahini, olive oil, lemon juice, garlic, salt, and pepper.
2. Blend until smooth, adding water for desired consistency.
3. Serve with pita chips, vegetables, or as a sandwich spread.

Crispy Tacos

Ingredients:

- 12 corn tortillas
- 1 lb ground beef or turkey
- 1 taco seasoning packet
- Oil for frying
- Toppings: lettuce, tomatoes, cheese, salsa

Instructions:

1. In a skillet, cook ground meat with taco seasoning until browned.
2. In a separate pan, heat oil over medium heat.
3. Fry each tortilla until crispy, about 1 minute per side.
4. Fill each taco shell with cooked meat and desired toppings.

Fruit Salad

Ingredients:

- 2 cups mixed fresh fruits (like berries, melons, and grapes)
- 1 tbsp honey or agave syrup
- 1 tbsp lime or lemon juice
- Optional: fresh mint for garnish

Instructions:

1. In a large bowl, combine mixed fruits.
2. Drizzle with honey and lime juice, tossing gently to coat.
3. Serve immediately or chill in the refrigerator for 30 minutes.

Energy Bites

Ingredients:

- 1 cup rolled oats
- 1/2 cup peanut butter or almond butter
- 1/3 cup honey or maple syrup
- 1/2 cup chocolate chips or dried fruit
- 1/4 cup flaxseed or chia seeds

Instructions:

1. In a bowl, mix all ingredients until well combined.
2. Roll into small balls, about 1 inch in diameter.
3. Refrigerate for 30 minutes before serving.

Savory Muffins

Ingredients:

- 1 1/2 cups all-purpose flour
- 1 tbsp baking powder
- 1/2 tsp salt
- 1 cup shredded cheese (like cheddar)
- 1/2 cup cooked vegetables (like spinach or bell peppers)
- 1 cup milk
- 1/4 cup olive oil
- 2 eggs

Instructions:

1. Preheat the oven to 400°F (200°C) and line a muffin tin.
2. In a bowl, combine flour, baking powder, and salt.
3. In another bowl, whisk together milk, oil, and eggs.
4. Combine wet and dry ingredients, then fold in cheese and vegetables.
5. Fill muffin cups and bake for 15-20 minutes until golden.

Frozen Smoothie Packs

Ingredients:

- 2 cups mixed frozen fruits (like berries and bananas)
- 1 cup spinach or kale (optional)
- 1/2 cup yogurt or non-dairy alternative
- 1/2 cup liquid (like almond milk or coconut water)

Instructions:

1. In zip-top bags, portion out frozen fruits and spinach (if using).
2. Seal and freeze for easy smoothie prep.
3. When ready to blend, add contents to a blender with yogurt and liquid, and blend until smooth.

Coconut Rice

Ingredients:

- 1 cup jasmine rice
- 1 cup coconut milk
- 1/2 cup water
- 1/2 tsp salt

Instructions:

1. Rinse the jasmine rice under cold water until the water runs clear.
2. In a pot, combine rice, coconut milk, water, and salt.
3. Bring to a boil, then reduce heat to low and cover.
4. Cook for 15-20 minutes until rice is tender and liquid is absorbed. Fluff with a

Homemade Croutons

Ingredients:

- 4 cups bread, cubed (stale or fresh)
- 1/4 cup olive oil
- 1 tsp garlic powder
- 1 tsp Italian seasoning
- Salt and pepper to taste

Instructions:

1. Preheat the oven to 375°F (190°C).
2. In a large bowl, toss bread cubes with olive oil, garlic powder, Italian seasoning, salt, and pepper.
3. Spread the cubes in a single layer on a baking sheet.
4. Bake for 10-15 minutes, stirring halfway, until golden brown.

Veggie Burgers

Ingredients:

- 1 can (15 oz) black beans, drained and rinsed
- 1 cup cooked quinoa
- 1/2 cup breadcrumbs
- 1/2 cup diced vegetables (like bell peppers and onions)
- 1 tsp garlic powder
- 1 tsp cumin
- Salt and pepper to taste

Instructions:

1. In a bowl, mash black beans with a fork.
2. Add cooked quinoa, breadcrumbs, diced vegetables, garlic powder, cumin, salt, and pepper.
3. Mix until combined and form into patties.
4. Cook in a skillet over medium heat for 4-5 minutes per side until heated through.

Noodle Salad

Ingredients:

- 8 oz noodles (like rice or soba)
- 1 cup mixed vegetables (like carrots, bell peppers, and cucumber)
- 1/4 cup soy sauce
- 2 tbsp sesame oil
- 1 tbsp rice vinegar
- Optional: sesame seeds and green onions for garnish

Instructions:

1. Cook noodles according to package instructions and drain.
2. In a large bowl, combine cooked noodles, mixed vegetables, soy sauce, sesame oil, and rice vinegar.
3. Toss to combine and serve chilled or at room temperature.
4. Garnish with sesame seeds and green onions if desired.

Fruit Infused Water

Ingredients:

- 1 pitcher of water
- 1 cup mixed fruits (like berries, citrus, or melon)
- Optional: herbs (like mint or basil)

Instructions:

1. Add mixed fruits and herbs to a pitcher of water.
2. Let infuse in the refrigerator for at least 1 hour.
3. Serve chilled and enjoy a refreshing drink.

Nut Milk

Ingredients:

- 1 cup nuts (like almonds, cashews, or hazelnuts)
- 4 cups water
- Sweetener to taste (like honey or maple syrup)
- Optional: vanilla extract

Instructions:

1. Soak nuts in water for at least 4 hours or overnight.
2. Drain and rinse the nuts, then blend with 4 cups of fresh water until smooth.
3. Strain through a nut milk bag or cheesecloth to separate the liquid from the pulp.
4. Sweeten to taste and store in the refrigerator for up to 3-4 days.

Pickles

Ingredients:

- 4 cups cucumber, sliced
- 1 cup white vinegar
- 1 cup water
- 2 tbsp salt
- 1 tbsp sugar
- 1 tbsp dill (fresh or dried)

Instructions:

1. In a saucepan, combine vinegar, water, salt, sugar, and dill.
2. Bring to a boil, then remove from heat and let cool.
3. Pack cucumber slices into a jar and pour the cooled brine over them.
4. Seal and refrigerate for at least 24 hours before enjoying.

Cake Pops

Ingredients:

- 1 box cake mix (any flavor)
- 1 can (16 oz) frosting (any flavor)
- 1 cup chocolate chips (for coating)
- Optional: sprinkles for decoration

Instructions:

1. Bake the cake according to package instructions and let cool.
2. Crumble the cake into a large bowl and mix in the frosting until combined.
3. Form mixture into small balls and place on a baking sheet.
4. Freeze for 1 hour to set.
5. Melt chocolate chips in a microwave-safe bowl.
6. Dip the end of a lollipop stick into the melted chocolate, then insert into each cake ball.
7. Dip each cake pop into the melted chocolate and decorate with sprinkles.

Herb Butter

Ingredients:

- 1 cup unsalted butter, softened
- 1/4 cup fresh herbs (like parsley, chives, or thyme), finely chopped
- 1 clove garlic, minced (optional)
- Salt and pepper to taste

Instructions:

1. In a bowl, combine softened butter, chopped herbs, garlic, salt, and pepper.
2. Mix until well combined.
3. Transfer to parchment paper, roll into a log, and refrigerate until firm.
4. Slice and use on bread, vegetables, or meats.
5. fork before serving.

Savory Rice Cakes

Ingredients:

- 2 cups cooked rice (white or brown)
- 1/2 cup grated cheese (like cheddar or mozzarella)
- 1/4 cup green onions, chopped
- 1/4 cup grated carrots
- 1 egg, beaten
- Salt and pepper to taste

Instructions:

1. In a bowl, combine cooked rice, cheese, green onions, carrots, beaten egg, salt, and pepper.
2. Mix until well combined.
3. Heat a non-stick skillet over medium heat and add a little oil.
4. Scoop 1/4 cup of the mixture into the skillet, flattening it slightly to form a cake.
5. Cook for about 3-4 minutes on each side until golden brown.
6. Repeat with the remaining mixture and serve warm.

Baked Goods

Ingredients:

- 2 cups all-purpose flour
- 1 cup sugar
- 1/2 cup butter, softened
- 1 cup milk
- 2 eggs
- 2 tsp baking powder
- 1 tsp vanilla extract
- Optional: chocolate chips or nuts

Instructions:

1. Preheat the oven to 350°F (175°C) and grease a baking dish.
2. In a bowl, cream together butter and sugar until light and fluffy.
3. Add eggs, milk, and vanilla, mixing well.
4. In another bowl, combine flour and baking powder, then gradually add to the wet ingredients.
5. Stir in chocolate chips or nuts if desired.
6. Pour into the prepared baking dish and bake for 25-30 minutes or until golden brown.

Egg Drop Soup

Ingredients:

- 4 cups chicken or vegetable broth
- 2 eggs, beaten
- 1/2 tsp cornstarch (optional, for thickening)
- 1 tsp soy sauce
- 1/2 tsp sesame oil
- Green onions for garnish

Instructions:

1. In a pot, bring the broth to a boil.
2. If using cornstarch, mix it with a little cold water to create a slurry and add it to the boiling broth.
3. Stir the soup and slowly drizzle in the beaten eggs while stirring continuously.
4. Add soy sauce and sesame oil.
5. Remove from heat, garnish with green onions, and serve hot.

Homemade Dog Treats

Ingredients:

- 2 cups whole wheat flour
- 1/2 cup peanut butter (unsweetened)
- 1/2 cup pumpkin puree
- 1/4 cup water (as needed)

Instructions:

1. Preheat the oven to 350°F (175°C).
2. In a bowl, combine flour, peanut butter, and pumpkin puree.
3. Gradually add water until the dough comes together.
4. Roll out the dough to 1/4 inch thick and cut into desired shapes.
5. Place on a baking sheet and bake for 20-25 minutes until golden.
6. Let cool before serving to your dog.

Potato Pancakes

Ingredients:

- 2 cups grated potatoes (about 2 medium potatoes)
- 1/2 cup onion, grated
- 1 egg, beaten
- 1/4 cup flour
- Salt and pepper to taste
- Oil for frying

Instructions:

1. In a bowl, combine grated potatoes, onion, beaten egg, flour, salt, and pepper.
2. Heat oil in a skillet over medium heat.
3. Drop spoonfuls of the mixture into the skillet, flattening them slightly.
4. Cook for 3-4 minutes on each side until crispy and golden brown.
5. Drain on paper towels and serve hot with sour cream or applesauce.

Stuffed Zucchini

Ingredients:

- 4 medium zucchinis, halved and scooped out
- 1 cup cooked quinoa or rice
- 1/2 cup diced tomatoes
- 1/2 cup shredded cheese
- 1/4 cup chopped basil or parsley
- Salt and pepper to taste

Instructions:

1. Preheat the oven to 375°F (190°C).
2. In a bowl, mix cooked quinoa or rice, diced tomatoes, cheese, herbs, salt, and pepper.
3. Stuff each zucchini half with the mixture.
4. Place in a baking dish and cover with foil.
5. Bake for 25-30 minutes until the zucchini is tender.

Chowder

Ingredients:

- 4 cups vegetable or chicken broth
- 2 cups diced potatoes
- 1 cup corn (fresh or frozen)
- 1 cup diced onion
- 1 cup milk or cream
- 2 tbsp butter
- Salt and pepper to taste

Instructions:

1. In a pot, melt butter over medium heat and sauté onions until translucent.
2. Add diced potatoes and broth, bringing to a boil.
3. Reduce heat and simmer until potatoes are tender, about 15 minutes.

4. Stir in corn and milk or cream, seasoning with salt and pepper.
5. Cook for an additional 5 minutes and serve hot.

Fruit Leather

Ingredients:

- 2 cups pureed fruit (like strawberries or apples)
- 1-2 tbsp honey or agave syrup (optional)
- 1 tbsp lemon juice

Instructions:

1. Preheat the oven to 170°F (75°C) or use a dehydrator.
2. In a bowl, mix fruit puree, honey (if using), and lemon juice.
3. Spread the mixture onto a parchment-lined baking sheet in a thin, even layer.
4. Bake for 6-8 hours or until the fruit leather is dry and not sticky.
5. Allow to cool, then cut into strips and roll up in parchment paper for storage.

Frozen Snacks

Ingredients:

- 2 cups yogurt (Greek or regular)
- 1 cup mixed berries (fresh or frozen)
- 1/4 cup honey or maple syrup
- 1/2 cup granola (optional)

Instructions:

1. In a bowl, mix yogurt and honey or maple syrup until well combined.
2. Fold in mixed berries.
3. Line a baking sheet with parchment paper.
4. Spoon the yogurt mixture onto the baking sheet, spreading it out evenly.
5. Sprinkle granola on top if desired.
6. Freeze for at least 4 hours or until solid.
7. Once frozen, break into pieces and store in an airtight container in the freezer.

Scones

Ingredients:

- 2 cups all-purpose flour
- 1/4 cup sugar
- 1 tbsp baking powder
- 1/2 tsp salt
- 1/2 cup butter, cold and cubed
- 1/2 cup milk
- 1 tsp vanilla extract
- Optional: dried fruits or chocolate chips

Instructions:

1. Preheat the oven to 400°F (200°C) and line a baking sheet with parchment paper.
2. In a large bowl, mix flour, sugar, baking powder, and salt.
3. Cut in the cold butter until the mixture resembles coarse crumbs.
4. Stir in milk and vanilla until just combined.
5. If desired, fold in dried fruits or chocolate chips.
6. Turn the dough onto a floured surface and knead gently.
7. Pat into a circle about 1 inch thick and cut into wedges.
8. Place on the baking sheet and bake for 15-20 minutes until golden brown.

Savory Rice Pilaf

Ingredients:

- 1 cup rice (white or brown)
- 2 cups vegetable or chicken broth
- 1/2 cup onion, chopped
- 1/2 cup carrots, diced
- 1/2 cup peas (fresh or frozen)
- 2 tbsp olive oil
- 1 tsp garlic powder
- Salt and pepper to taste

Instructions:

1. In a pot, heat olive oil over medium heat.
2. Add onions and carrots, sautéing until softened.
3. Stir in the rice and garlic powder, cooking for another minute.
4. Pour in the broth, bringing it to a boil.
5. Reduce heat to low, cover, and simmer for 15-20 minutes or until rice is cooked.
6. Stir in peas, season with salt and pepper, and serve warm.

www.ingramcontent.com/pod-product-compliance
Lightning Source LLC
LaVergne TN
LVHW061957070526
838199LV00060B/4177